My thanks to the following aquatic ecologists:
Steven Ray Zimmerman; Dr. Brooks M. Burr, Professor at Southern Illinois University Carbondale;
Ashley Moerke; and Dr. Gary A. Lamberti, Professor at the University of Notre Dame.

For Turner Willett,
awesome nephew and pond digger

—A. P. S.

To my own little school of minnows,
Sumner, Hampton, Lawson, and Cameron

—T. P.

The illustrations were created digitally on a Macintosh using Fractal Design's Painter
The text and display type were set in Pike and Funhouse
Composed in the United States of America
Designed by Lois A. Rainwater
Edited by Aimee Jackson

Text © 2004 by April Pulley Sayre
Illustrations © 2004 by Trip Park

NORTHWORD

Books for Young Readers
11571 K- Tel Drive
Minnetonka, MN 55343
www.tnkidsbooks.com

Library of Congress Cataloging-in-Publication Data

Sayre, April Pulley.
Trout, trout, trout! : a fish chant / by April Pulley Sayre ; illustrated by Trip Park.
p.   cm.
Summary: Presents a rhyme and information about a variety of freshwater fish found in
North America north of Mexico.
ISBN 1-55971-889-7
1. Freshwater fishes—North America—Juvenile literature. [1. Freshwater fishes. 2.
Fishes.] I. Park, Trip, ill. II. Title.

QL625.S28 2004

597.176'0973—dc21   2003052720

Printed in Singapore
10 9 8 7 6 5 4 3

TROUT, TROUT, TROUT! (A FISH CHANT)

BY APRIL PULLEY SAYRE

ILLUSTRATED BY TRIP PARK

NorthWord
Minnetonka, Minnesota

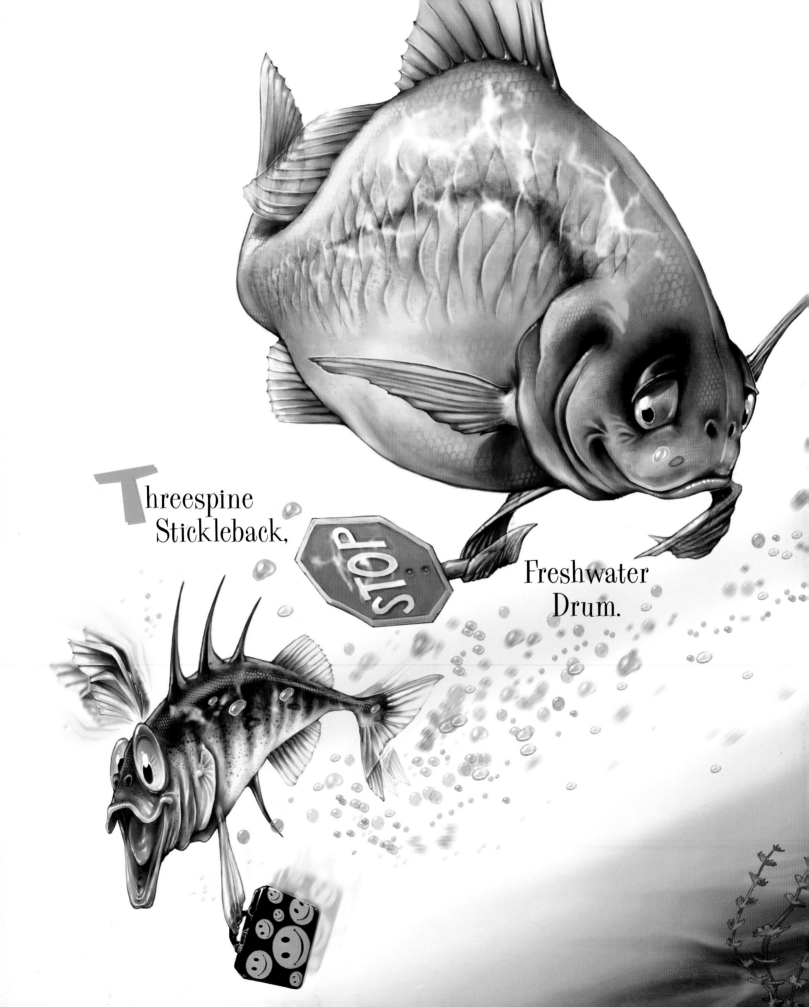

Threespine Stickleback,

Freshwater Drum.

Lake Chub,   Creek Chub,

Chum,
Chum,
Chum.

Sockeye
Salmon,

Arctic Char,

Mooneye, Walleye, Gar, Gar, Gar!

Rainbow Shiner, lookin' sharp.

Whitefish,

Goldfish,
　　Carp, Carp, Carp!

Paddlefish,
Flagfish,
they're all real.

Mosquitofish, Sunfish,

Eel, Eel, Eel!

Shovelnose Sturgeon,
love that face.
Spoonhead Sculpin,

Dace, Dace, Dace!

Bigmouth Buffalo,
California Roach.

Frecklebelly Madtom, Loach, Loach, Loach!

Popeye Shiner, he looks mad.

Stonecat,

Blindcat,

Shad,
Shad,
Shad!

Waccamaw Killifish, see it pass?
Largescale Stoneroller,

River
Redhorse,
gotta' search!

Pygmy Sunfish,

Perch, Perch, Perch!

Chestnut Lamprey,
lookin' odd.

Pupfish,   Catfish,

Cod,
Cod,
Cod!

Yazoo Darter, shout it out!

Cavefish,

Swampfish,

Trout,
Trout,
Trout!

Starhead Topminnow,

Northern Pike.

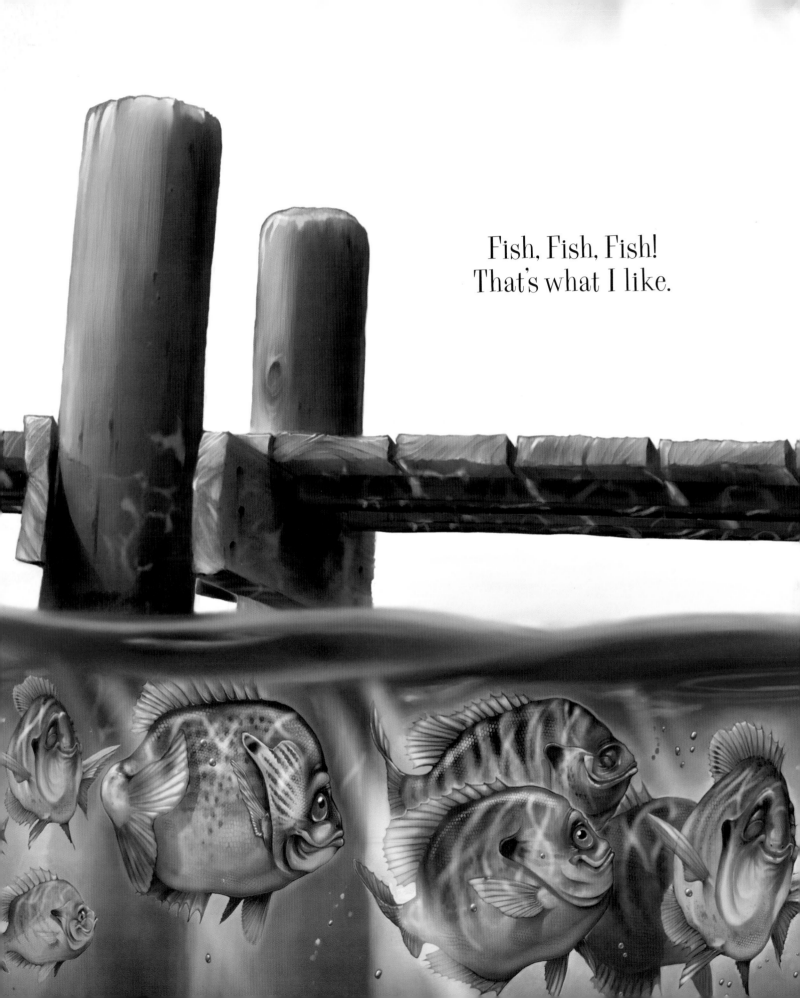

Fish, Fish, Fish!
That's what I like.

HOORAY FOR AMERICAN FISH!

 All the fish in this book are freshwater fish found in North America, north of Mexico. They inhabit ponds, lakes, streams, and rivers. Most are native to the United States and Canada, meaning that they were here before humans came along. A few, such as carp, were released in American waters by people. But those fish now live and reproduce in the wild in some areas.

THREESPINE STICKLEBACK

Stickleback are named for the spines on their backs. Count the spines to find out if it's a threespine, fourspine, or a ninespine stickleback. Stickleback live in shallows of ponds, lakes, or streams.

FRESHWATER DRUM

Freshwater drum are named for the loud, drum-like sounds they make underwater. Scientists believe that the drum sounds are some kind of mating call. Drum live in lakes and rivers.

LAKE CHUB

Chub is a general term used for many different species of minnow. There are over 2,000 kinds of minnow worldwide. Lake chub live in Alaska, Canada, and the Great Lakes. You can tell a chub from other minnows by the barbel (the mustache-like feeler) that sticks out of each corner of its mouth.

CREEK CHUB

Creek chub live in rocky and sandy pools in creeks and small rivers. The males dig a pit in the sand or gravel. There the female lays eggs. The male guards these eggs until they hatch.

CHUM

Chum is any fish that is used as bait to catch other fish. There is also a fish called the chum salmon.

SOCKEYE SALMON

Sockeye salmon, also known as red salmon, hatch from eggs in rivers in Alaska and northern California. They swim to the ocean, grow larger, and then after several years, swim back into the rivers to spawn. Spawning is the process of female fish laying eggs and male fish fertilizing the eggs.

ARCTIC CHAR

Arctic char is one of the most northern fish. It lives in deeper parts of rivers and also in lakes. Individual char vary in color.

MOONEYE

Mooneye have large eyes that are yellow, like the moon. They eat insects and small fish. They let their eggs float along on the surface of streams and lakes. They live in the Great Lakes.

WALLEYE

Walleye have silvery, clouded eyes that help them see in low light. They live in lakes and rivers. Walleye are popular sport fish, meaning anglers like to catch them.

GAR

With toothy jaws and long snouts, gar look like no other fish. Seven species of gar inhabit North America. These primitive fish live in swamps, lakes, and near the edges of rivers.

RAINBOW SHINER

Shiners are minnows. Rainbow shiner live in small streams in the southeastern United States. The male is especially brightly colored during breeding season.

WHITEFISH

Whitefish are in the same family as trout, salmon, and char: *Salmonidae*. There are many species of whitefish. The lake whitefish lives in the Great Lakes and is a popular food fish.

GOLDFISH

Goldfish are native to Asia. But many now live in North American waters. For hundreds of years, people have released them into the wild. Releasing pet store fish is not recommended because they may compete with or introduce disease to wild fish. Many goldfish are not actually gold, but are varied in color.

CARP

Carp look like goldfish except for the barbels near their mouths. They were brought from Europe to America in the late 1880s as a type of fish for ponds. When ponds overflowed from rain, the carp made their way into wild streams, ponds, and lakes.

PADDLEFISH

The paddlefish has a snout shaped like the paddle of a canoe. It lives in the deep waters of the Mississippi and Missouri Rivers. Paddlefish are a primitive type of fish that can grow to be 7 feet (2.1 meters) long. The paddle has taste buds on its underside that help the fish find food.

FLAGFISH

Flagfish belong to the same family as pupfish. Flagfish live only in Florida in lakes, ponds, and streams.

MOSQUITOFISH

These small fish are native to ponds, lakes, and pools along streams in the eastern United States. They get their name from their habit of eating mosquito larvae. They have been released into some areas for mosquito control. Unlike many fish, mosquitofish give birth to live young. They do not lay eggs.

SUNFISH

Sunfish belong to the same family as bass. There are many species of sunfish, such as the bluegill, pumpkinseed, and redear sunfish. Most sunfish build nests near the shores of streams and ponds.

EEL

Eels look a lot like snakes. American eels hatch from eggs in the Atlantic Ocean. Then they swim to the coast of the United States and up into streams. Later, the adult male and female fish will travel back out into the ocean to spawn.

SHOVELNOSE STURGEON

Shovelnose sturgeon are named for their shovel-like nose. These large, primitive fish live in the Mississippi River basin. Other species of sturgeon live in Europe. Sturgeon can grow to be 15 feet (4.6 meters) long, from head to tail!

SPOONHEAD SCULPIN

Spoonhead sculpin have wide, flat heads and prickly spines. These northern fish are found in the Great Lakes, and in rivers as far south as Ohio.

MORE AMERICAN FISH!

DACE

Dace is a name used for many fish in the minnow family. Longfin dace, desert dace, and redfin dace are just a few of these minnow species. Dace are small, generally less than 5 inches (12.7 centimeters) long.

POPEYE SHINER

The popeye shiner is named for its huge eyes. These rare fish live in the Ohio River basin, in the gravelly pools formed by streams.

STONECAT

Whiskers are one reason that stonecats are a member of the bullhead catfish family. Stonecats live in streams from the Great Lakes to Alabama.

BLINDCAT

There are two species of blindcat: toothless and widemouth. Both the widemouth blindcats and the toothless blindcats live underground in water that flows through caves near San Antonio, Texas. They don't need eyes because they live in the dark.

SHAD

Shad are silvery fish. Some live in estuaries where rivers meet the sea and freshwater and saltwater mix. Like salmon, shad swim up streams to spawn.

BIGMOUTH BUFFALO

Bigmouth buffalo are members of the sucker family. Suckers slurp small, aquatic insects off the bottom of lakes and streams. In addition to the bigmouth buffalo, there is also a smallmouth buffalo.

CALIFORNIA ROACH

This fish lives in rocky pools of rivers and streams only in California. It only grows to be about 4 inches (10.2 centimeters) long.

FRECKLEBELLY MADTOM

Named for the spots on its belly, this fish lives in rivers in Georgia, Alabama, Louisiana, and Mississippi. Don't touch these fish without proper supervision. Madtom, like other catfish, have glands that give off a poison that stings.

LOACH

Loach are fish sold for aquariums. They are native to Eurasia and Africa. But one type of loach, the oriental weatherfish, has been released into wild streams in several parts of the United States and now lives in the wild.

WACCAMAW KILLIFISH

This fish is native to Lake Waccamaw, in North Carolina. They swim close to the water's surface. They only grow to be 4 inches (10.2 centimeters) long.

LARGESCALE STONEROLLER

Largescale stonerollers scrape algae off of rocks by using their hard lower jaws. Largescale stonerollers are in the minnow family and live in the eastern and midwestern United States.

BASS

There are many kinds of bass: largemouth, smallmouth, redeye, and others. Male bass fan their fins to swirl away the sand at the edge of a pond, stream, or lake. This creates a hollow, or nest, where the female lays eggs.

RIVER REDHORSE

River redhorse live in the rivers of the midwestern and eastern United States. They are members of the sucker family.

PYGMY SUNFISH

Pygmy sunfish are in a family of fish that includes the banded pygmy sunfish, okefenokee pygmy sunfish, and others. True to their name, they are small—less than 2 inches (5.1 centimeters) in length.

PERCH

Over 150 North American fish species belong to the perch family: *Percidae*. It includes darters, walleyes, perch, and saugers.

CHESTNUT LAMPREY

Lampreys look a lot like eels. Some lamprey species use their sucker mouths to attach to larger fish and feed off them.

PUPFISH

Most pupfish live in streams, marshes, and springs, in the southwestern deserts. Many pupfish are rare, partly because each species lives in only a few locations. When these habitats are threatened, the pupfish become endangered.

CATFISH

Catfish are named for their whiskers. There are thousands of catfish species worldwide; 44 species live in the United States.

COD

Most cod are marine fish, meaning they live in the saltwater of the ocean. But two species, burbot and Atlantic tomcod, are found in North American rivers and lakes. The burbot has one long barbel hanging from its chin.

YAZOO DARTER

This tiny fish is found in the pools of small streams of the Yazoo River in Mississippi. It is only 2¼ inches (5.7 centimeters) long. Darters get their name because they dart around. Unlike most fish, if they stop swimming, they sink to the bottom.

CAVEFISH

Cavefish live in springs and streams in caves in the eastern United States. Some have no eyes and are pinkish or whitish. Cavefish have sensors on their fins that help them feel where they are in their dark cave habitat. Many cavefish are endangered.

SWAMPFISH

Swampfish are in the cavefish family. But swampfish live in swamps and streams out in the light. Swampfish have eyes and their scales are dark in color.

TROUT

Trout are in the *Salmonidae* family. They tend to live in cold streams and lakes. They have been introduced into many lakes and streams because they are a popular sport fish.

STARHEAD TOPMINNOW

The Starhead Topminnow gets its name from the gold spot on the top of its head and the fact that it feeds near the top of the water.

NORTHERN PIKE

These large, popular sport fish feed on other fish. They live in streams and lakes across much of northern North America. Northern pike can grow to be 4 feet (1.2 meters) long.

FISH, FISH, FISH! THAT'S WHAT I LIKE.

APRIL PULLEY SAYRE is the award-winning author of more than fifty books for young readers including *If You Should Hear a Honey Guide*; *Turtle, Turtle, Watch Out!*; and *River and Stream*. She has also written for *Ranger Rick* and *World*. Sayre's books, renowned for their lyricism, accuracy, and sometimes silliness, have been translated into French, Dutch, Japanese, and Korean. April really is interested in the ecology of freshwater fish, but she just can't stop laughing at their common names. For more information about April, visit her at: www.aprilsayre.com.

As a kid, TRIP PARK had every kind of aquarium fish, and with a pond in his yard and a lake in his town, he quickly became an amateur expert on his scaly friends. Trip was drawn to advertising, as an art director long before he illustrated, and his editorial cartoons have been in Greensboro's *News & Record* and *USA Today*. He also illustrated *Gopher Up Your Sleeve*, a children's picture book written by Tony Johnston. Trip currently resides in Charlotte, North Carolina, with his wife and his own school of four children.

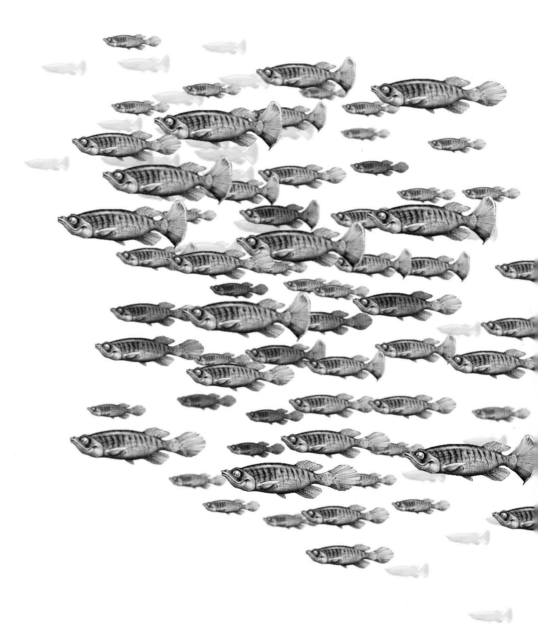